ONE YEAR TO WEALTH

A Blueprint for Financial Success

SOMUDEEP BHATTACHARJEE

Dedicated
to
My Beloved Parents

'Lack of knowledge exposes you to risk'

By Warren Buffett

TABLE OF CONTENTS

ACKNOWLEDGMENTS

Thank you to everyone who read my work and who contributed to my wonderful life. Thank you to all those people who transform the life of others by living as an example.

CHAPTER 1: INTRODUCTION

This chapter provides readers with an overview of the book's purpose and what they can expect to learn. The first part of the chapter explains the aim of the book, which is to provide readers with a step-by-step guide to achieving financial success in just one year. The authors emphasize the importance of financial stability and how this book can help readers achieve their financial goals.

The second part of the chapter provides an overview of the current financial landscape and the challenges individuals face in their quest for financial success. This section highlights the economic challenges of inflation, market volatility, and job security, which can make it difficult to create wealth. The authors also discuss the common challenges individuals face, such as debt, lack of financial knowledge, and insufficient income.

Despite these challenges, the authors emphasize that achieving financial success is possible with the right guidance and a well-defined plan. The following chapters will provide readers with practical advice and easy-to-follow steps to create a sustainable financial plan, generate multiple streams of income, and overcome common financial challenges.

1.1 Explanation of the purpose of the book and what readers can expect to learn

In today's world, financial stability and wealth creation are increasingly becoming essential for a secure and fulfilling life. However, achieving financial success can be a daunting task, especially in the phase of economic challenges and uncertainties. This book aims to provide you with a proven blueprint to achieving financial success in just one year.

The purpose of this book is to guide you towards financial freedom and help you achieve your financial goals. This book showcases the years of experience of many authors in finance for helping numerous individuals in achieving their financial dreams. We will provide you with practical advice and easy-to-follow steps that you can implement in your daily life to create a sustainable financial plan. In this book, you can expect to learn:

  ➤ The importance of setting specific financial goals and how to achieve them.
  ➤ How to create a budget and manage your finances effectively.
  ➤ The basics of investing and how to create a diversified investment portfolio.
  ➤ Strategies for building multiple streams of income and

generating passive income.

> Tips for staying motivated and overcoming common financial challenges.

By the end of this book, you will have a clear understanding of the steps you need to take to achieve financial success and create a secure financial future for yourself and your family.

1.2 Overview of the current financial landscape and the challenges facing individuals who want to become rich

The current financial landscape is characterized by economic challenges such as high inflation, volatile markets, and unpredictable job security. In such a scenario, achieving financial stability and creating wealth has become increasingly important.

However, the path to financial success is often filled with obstacles and setbacks, making it difficult for individuals to achieve their goals. High levels of debt, lack of financial knowledge, and insufficient income are some of the common challenges that individuals face.

Moreover, market volatility and unexpected expenses can make it difficult to achieve financial stability. The COVID-19 pandemic has highlighted the importance of having a robust financial plan in place to cope with unexpected events. Despite these challenges, it is still possible to achieve financial success with the right guidance and a well-defined plan. In the following chapters, we will guide you through the steps you can take to achieve your financial goals and become rich in just one year.

CHAPTER 2: SETTING FINANCIAL GOALS

This chapter is focused on the importance of setting specific, measurable, achievable, relevant, and time-bound (SMART) financial goals. The first part of the chapter explains why setting SMART goals are important for creating a solid financial plan. The authors highlight how having clear, achievable goals can help individuals prioritize their spending, save money, and invest in their future.

The second part of the chapter provides readers with a step-by-step guide to setting financial goals, including long-term and short-term goals. The guide emphasizes the importance of identifying financial priorities and values, breaking down long-term goals into short-term milestones, and setting SMART goals for each milestone. The authors also emphasize the importance of tracking progress and adjusting goals as necessary.

By the end of this chapter, readers will have a clear

understanding of why setting SMART financial goals is important and a practical guide to setting both long-term and short-term goals. This will help readers develop a solid foundation for achieving their financial objectives.

2.1 Explanation of the importance of setting specific, measurable, achievable, relevant, and time-bound (SMART) goals

Setting financial goals is the foundation of any successful financial plan. It helps individuals prioritize their spending, save money, and invest in their future. However, setting vague or unrealistic goals can hinder progress and lead to disappointment. This section emphasizes the importance of setting SMART goals that are Specific, Measurable, Achievable, Relevant, and Time-bound.

Setting specific goals helps individuals clarify their priorities and focus their efforts. Measurable goals enable individuals to track their progress and adjust their strategy if necessary. Achievable goals are realistic and attainable, while relevant goals are aligned with an individual's values and long-term objectives. Finally, time-bound goals have a deadline, which provides a sense of urgency and motivation.

2.2 Step-by-step guide to setting financial goals, including long-term and short-term goals

This section provides readers with a step-by-step guide to setting financial goals. It emphasizes the importance of setting both long-term and short-term goals. Long-term goals, such as retirement planning or buying a home, provide a sense of direction and purpose. Short-term goals, such as saving for a vacation or paying off credit card debt, provide motivation and a sense of accomplishment. The step-by-step guide includes the following:

- ➢ Identify your financial priorities and values
- ➢ Define your long-term financial goals
- ➢ Break down long-term goals into short-term milestones
- ➢ Set SMART goals for each milestone
- ➢ Track your progress and adjust your plan as necessary

The guide emphasizes the importance of reviewing and adjusting goals periodically. As circumstances change, priorities may shift, and goals may need to be revised. By the end of this chapter, readers will have a clear understanding of the importance of setting SMART financial goals and a practical guide to setting long-term and short-term goals.

CHAPTER 3: CREATING A BUDGET

This chapter provides readers with a comprehensive guide on creating a budget for achieving financial success. It highlights the importance of budgeting and provides a step-by-step guide on how to create a budget that fits readers' individual needs. The chapter also offers practical advice on reducing expenses, increasing income, and tracking expenses. By the end of the chapter, readers will have a solid understanding of how to develop and maintain an effective budget that will help them achieve their long-term financial goals.

3.1 The Importance of Budgeting for Achieving Financial Success

Creating and maintaining a budget is a crucial step towards achieving financial success. Budgeting helps individuals and households to manage their finances, set financial goals, and track their progress towards those goals. Some of the benefits of budgeting include:

- ➢ Helps to control spending and prevent overspending
- ➢ Enables you to save money and build wealth
- ➢ Provides clarity and awareness of your financial situation
- ➢ Helps to prioritize spending and identify areas where you can reduce expenses
- ➢ Reduces stress and uncertainty related to money management
- ➢ Enables you to plan for the future and work towards long-term financial goals

3.2 How to Create a Budget

Creating a budget involves a few key steps:

- ➢ **Step 1- Determine your monthly income:** The first step in creating a budget is to determine your monthly income. This includes all sources of income, such as your salary, bonuses, tips, and any other sources of income.

- ➢ **Step 2- List your monthly expenses:** The next step is to list all of your monthly expenses. This includes fixed expenses such as rent or mortgage payments, utilities, insurance, and car payments. It also includes variable expenses such as groceries, entertainment, and dining out.

➤ **Step 3- Categorize your expenses:** Once you have listed all of your expenses, categorize them into essential and non-essential expenses. Essential expenses are those that you must pay to live, such as rent, utilities, and food. Non-essential expenses are those that are optional, such as entertainment, hobbies, and dining out.

➤ **Step 4- Set a budget for each category:** After categorizing your expenses, set a budget for each category. Start with your essential expenses and allocate a specific amount for each category. For example, you may allocate 30% of your income to rent, 15% to utilities, and 10% to groceries. Next, allocate a specific amount for your non-essential expenses.

➤ **Step 5- Track your spending:** Once you have created a budget, it is important to track your spending to ensure that you are staying within your budget. Use a budgeting app or spreadsheet to track your expenses and adjust your budget as needed.

3.3   Tips for Reducing Expenses and Increasing Income

In addition to creating a budget, there are several tips you can use to reduce expenses and increase income, including:

➤ Reduce unnecessary expenses such as dining out or subscription services.

- ➢ Shop for deals and discounts when making purchases.
- ➢ Negotiate bills and expenses such as insurance and phone bills.
- ➢ Increase your income through part-time work or freelance jobs.
- ➢ Start a side business or sell unwanted items to earn extra income.

By following these tips and creating a budget, you can take control of your finances and work towards achieving your financial goals.

CHAPTER 4: INVESTING WISELY

This chapter provides an introduction to the basics of investing and offers tips for choosing investments and developing an investment strategy that aligns with personal financial goals. The chapter is divided into two parts, with Part 1 covering the types of investments, risk tolerance, and diversification. Part 2 offers guidance on understanding personal financial goals, time horizons, and how to choose investments that align with one's risk tolerance. The chapter emphasizes the importance of diversification and regular monitoring of investments, while also recommending the use of financial advisors for those who need assistance in developing an investment strategy.

4.1   Introduction to the Basics of Investing

Investing can be an excellent way to grow your wealth over time, but it can also be intimidating if you're not familiar with the basics. This part of the chapter will provide an overview of the types of investments available, how to assess your risk tolerance, and why diversification is important.

I) Types of Investments

There are several types of investments available, including stocks, bonds, mutual funds, exchange-traded funds (ETFs), real estate, and more. Each type of investment carries its own unique risks and rewards, and it's essential to understand the basics of each before investing.

II) Risk Tolerance

Your risk tolerance is the amount of risk you're comfortable taking on when investing. It's essential to understand your risk tolerance, as investing always involves some degree of risk. By knowing your risk tolerance, you can make more informed investment decisions that align with your financial goals and comfort level.

III) Diversification

Diversification is an investment strategy that involves spreading your money across multiple investments to minimize risk. By diversifying your portfolio, you can reduce the impact of any single investment's performance on your overall portfolio.

4.2 Tips for Choosing Investments and Developing an Investment Strategy

Now that you understand the basics of investing, it's time to develop an investment strategy that aligns with your personal financial goals. This part of the chapter will provide tips for choosing investments and developing an investment strategy that works for you.

I)   Understand Your Goals

The first step in developing an investment strategy is to understand your financial goals. Do you want to save for retirement, buy a house, or pay for your children's education? By understanding your goals, you can make more informed investment decisions that align with your long-term financial plans.

II)   Consider Your Time Horizon

Your time horizon is the length of time you plan to hold your investments. If you're investing for retirement, your time horizon may be several decades, while investing for a shorter-term goal may have a time horizon of a few years. Understanding your time horizon can help you choose investments that align with your goals.

III)   Choose Investments that Align with Your Risk Tolerance

As discussed in Part 1, your risk tolerance is an essential factor in choosing investments. It's crucial to select investments that align with your risk tolerance, as investing too aggressively or too conservatively can negatively impact your portfolio's performance.

IV) Diversify Your Portfolio

Diversification is crucial to any investment strategy. By spreading your money across different investments, you can minimize risk and maximize potential returns. Consider diversifying your portfolio across different asset classes, such as stocks, bonds, and real estate, and across different industries.

V) Monitor Your Investments

Investing is not a "set it and forget it" strategy. It's essential to monitor your investments regularly to ensure they continue to align with your financial goals and risk tolerance. Consider reviewing your portfolio at least once a year and making adjustments as necessary.

4.3 Summary:

Investing can be an excellent way to grow your wealth over time, but it's crucial to understand the basics and develop an investment strategy that aligns with your personal financial goals. By considering your goals, time horizon, risk tolerance, and diversification, you can make more informed investment decisions and maximize your potential returns while minimizing risk. Remember to monitor your investments regularly and make adjustments as necessary to ensure your portfolio continues to align with your financial goals.

CHAPTER 5: BUILDING MULTIPLE STREAMS OF INCOME

This chapter is divided into two parts; the first part discusses the benefits of having multiple sources of income, including financial security, faster achievement of financial goals, and more freedom and flexibility. The second part provides ideas for creating additional streams of income, such as freelancing, entrepreneurship, passive income strategies, and rental income. The chapter concludes by emphasizing the importance of diversifying your sources of revenue to achieve financial security and independence.

5.1   Benefits of having multiple sources of income

Having multiple streams of income is crucial for financial stability and independence. Relying on a single source of income is not only risky but can also limit your earning potential. By building multiple streams of income, you can diversify your sources of revenue and increase your overall income.

One of the significant benefits of having multiple streams of income is that it can provide you with financial security. If one of your income sources dries up or experiences a downturn, you will still have other sources of revenue to rely on. This can help you avoid financial stress and weather any financial storms that come your way.

Another advantage of having multiple streams of income is that it can help you achieve your financial goals faster. When you have more than one income source, you can earn more money and invest it to create even more income streams. This compounding effect can help you reach your financial goals faster than relying on a single source of income.

5.2   Ideas for Creating Additional Streams of Income

There are many ways to create additional streams of income. In this section, we will explore some of the most popular strategies, including freelancing, entrepreneurship, and passive income strategies.

I)   **Freelancing**: Freelancing is an excellent way to earn extra income by using your skills and expertise. You can offer your services as a freelancer in various areas, such as writing, designing, programming, and consulting. Freelancing allows you to work on projects that interest you and set your own schedule. There are many online platforms, such as Upwork, Fiverr, and Freelancer, where you can find freelance work.

II) **Entrepreneurship:** Starting a business is a fantastic way to create an additional stream of income. You can start a business in an area that interests you and leverage your skills and experience to build a successful enterprise. Entrepreneurship can be challenging, but it can also be highly rewarding if done right. You can start a business online or offline, depending on your interests and resources.

III) **Passive Income Strategies:** Passive income strategies involve earning money without actively working for it. This can include investing in stocks, real estate, or other assets that generate income. You can also create passive income streams through digital products, such as e-books, courses, and membership sites. Building a passive income stream may take some time, effort, and money upfront, but it can provide a steady source of income in the long run.

IV) **Rental Income:** Rental income is a popular way to generate passive income. You can rent out a property that you own, such as a vacation home or investment property. Rental income can provide a steady source of revenue, and you can hire a property manager to handle the day-to-day operations.

However, becoming a landlord comes with responsibilities and risks, so you should do your research before investing in rental properties.

5.3 Summary:

Building multiple streams of income is essential for financial security and independence. By diversifying your sources of revenue, you can increase your earning potential and achieve your financial goals faster. There are various ways to create additional streams of income, including freelancing, entrepreneurship, and passive income strategies. Choose the strategies that work best for you and start building your multiple streams of income today.

CHAPTER 6: STAYING MOTIVATED AND OVERCOMING CHALLENGES

This chapter is titled "Staying Motivated and Overcoming Challenges" and is divided into two parts. The first part provides strategies for staying motivated and maintaining momentum on the path to financial success. These include defining your goals, celebrating small wins, surrounding yourself with positivity, finding inspiration, and continuously learning. The second part focuses on tips for overcoming common challenges and setbacks, such as debt, unexpected expenses, market volatility, lack of progress, and burnout. The chapter emphasizes the importance of staying focused, reassessing your strategy when necessary, and pushing forward towards your financial goals.

6.1 Strategies for staying motivated and maintaining momentum on the path to financial success

Staying motivated is crucial when it comes to achieving financial success. It can be easy to get discouraged when you encounter setbacks, but it's important to stay focused on your goals and keep pushing forward. Here are some strategies for staying motivated:

I) **Define your goals:** To stay motivated, you need to have a clear idea of what you're working towards. Write down your financial goals, both short-term and long-term. This will give you something to focus on and help you measure your progress.

II) **Celebrate small wins:** It's important to acknowledge and celebrate your achievements, no matter how small they may be. This can help you stay motivated and maintain momentum.

III) **Surround yourself with positivity:** The people you surround yourself with can have a big impact on your mindset. Make sure you spend time with people who are supportive and positive. This can help you stay motivated and feel more confident in your abilities.

IV) **Find inspiration:** Look for role models and success stories that inspire you. This can help you stay motivated and remind you of what's possible.

V) Keep learning: The more you learn about personal finance and investing, the more confident you'll feel. This can help you stay motivated and make better financial decisions.

6.2 Tips for overcoming common challenges and setbacks, such as debt, unexpected expenses, and market volatility

Even with the best intentions and strategies, you're likely to encounter setbacks and challenges along the way. Here are some tips for overcoming common financial challenges:

I) Debt: If you're struggling with debt, it's important to tackle it head-on. Create a plan for paying off your debt, and consider working with a financial advisor or credit counselor to get help.

II) Unexpected expenses: It's always a good idea to have an emergency fund in place to cover unexpected expenses. If you don't have one, start building one now. You can also consider taking out insurance policies to protect against unexpected expenses.

III) Market volatility: The stock market can be unpredictable, and market volatility can be unsettling. The key is to stay calm and stick to your long-term investment strategy. Avoid making impulsive decisions based on short-term market fluctuations.

IV) **Lack of progress**: If you feel like you're not making progress towards your financial goals, it's important to reassess your strategy. Consider seeking help from a financial advisor or mentor who can help you identify areas where you can improve.

V) **Burnout:** It's easy to get burned out when you're working hard towards a goal. Make sure you take time for self-care and relaxation to avoid burnout. This can help you stay motivated and maintain momentum towards your financial goals.

6.3 Summary:

Staying motivated and overcoming challenges are critical to achieving financial success. By implementing the strategies and tips outlined in this chapter, you can stay on track and achieve your financial goals. Remember to stay focused, celebrate small wins, and surround yourself with positivity. And when you encounter setbacks or challenges, don't get discouraged – stay calm, reassess your strategy, and keep pushing forward.

CHAPTER 7: CONCLUSION

The purpose of this book was to provide readers with practical tips and advice on how to become rich and achieve financial success. In today's financial landscape, many challenges can hinder individuals from achieving their financial goals. However, by following the steps outlined in this book, readers can create a solid foundation for their financial future.

The first step towards financial success is setting specific, measurable, achievable, relevant, and time-bound (SMART) goals. This includes both long-term and short-term goals that are realistic and achievable.

Creating a budget is another important step in achieving financial success. It helps individuals track their spending, reduce expenses, and increase their income. Investing wisely is also essential, and readers should develop an investment strategy that aligns with their personal financial goals.

Building multiple streams of income can also be beneficial, and readers should consider different strategies such as freelancing, entrepreneurship, and passive income.

Staying motivated and overcoming challenges is crucial when it comes to achieving financial success. Readers should surround themselves with positivity, celebrate small wins, and seek help when necessary.

In conclusion, the journey towards financial success is not an easy one, but it is achievable with the right mindset, tools, and strategies. By setting SMART goals, creating a budget, investing wisely, building multiple streams of income, and staying motivated, readers can pave the way towards a financially secure future. Remember to remain persistent, seek help when needed, and never give up on your dreams.

FEW SHORT MOTIVATIONAL STORIES OF RICH INDIVIDUALS

I) Homemade candles Business

Sarah had always been interested in entrepreneurship, but she never had the courage to take the leap. She had a steady job at a retail store, but it barely paid her bills. She would spend her free time scrolling through social media, watching videos of people starting their own businesses and becoming successful. One day, Sarah stumbled upon a video of a woman who made homemade candles and sold them online. Intrigued, Sarah did some research and realized that there was a huge demand for handmade candles. She decided to give it a try and started making candles in her spare time. At first, Sarah struggled to sell her candles. She would post pictures of them on social media, but no one seemed interested. Discouraged, she almost gave up. But then, she discovered Etsy, an online marketplace for handmade goods. She created an account and started listing her candles. To her surprise, her candles started selling like hotcakes. People loved the unique scents and the beautiful packaging. Sarah was overwhelmed by the response and decided to focus all her energy on her candle business. She started experimenting with new scents and designs and even created a website to showcase her products. She spent countless hours perfecting her craft and promoting her business on social media. Within a few months, Sarah's business had taken off. She was receiving orders from all over the world and had even hired a few employees to help her with production. She was making more money than she ever thought possible and was well on her way to achieving financial freedom. By the end of the year, Sarah had made over $100,000 from her candle business. She had enough savings to quit her day job and focus on her business full-time. She felt grateful for the journey and the lessons learned along the way. She realized that with hard work, determination, and a little bit of luck, anyone could achieve financial success.

II) Stock market

Tom was a recent college graduate with a degree in finance. He had always been fascinated by the stock market and had a passion for investing. However, he didn't have much money to invest as he had just started his first job as a financial analyst. One day, Tom stumbled upon a Reddit forum where people were discussing high-risk stocks with potentially high returns. Intrigued, he decided to do some research and chose a few stocks that he believed had the potential to make a significant profit. He invested all his savings into those stocks, which was a risky move considering that he had very little experience in investing. The first few weeks were nerve-wracking as the stocks fluctuated dramatically. However, to his surprise, the stocks began to rise, and he was making a profit. Encouraged by his success, Tom continued to invest in more high-risk stocks, and his portfolio continued to grow. He would spend hours reading financial news and analyzing data to make informed decisions about his investments. Within a few months, Tom's portfolio had grown significantly, and he had made a substantial profit. He had managed to turn his initial investment of a few thousand dollars into tens of thousands. Tom was thrilled with his success and decided to take his investing to the next level. He started investing in more stable and diversified portfolios and continued to make smart investment decisions. He even started a blog to share his investment strategies and tips with others who were interested in the stock market. By the end of the year, Tom had made so much money that he could quit his job and focus on investing full-time. He had become a millionaire in just one year, and his success had even caught the attention of some of the top investment firms in the country. Tom realized that with a little bit of courage and a lot of hard work, anyone could achieve financial success.

III) Art work and Social Media

Emily was a struggling artist. She had just graduated from art school and was working a part-time job at a local coffee shop to make ends meet. Emily had always dreamed of becoming a successful artist, but she had never been able to get her work noticed by the right people. One day, Emily was browsing social media when she stumbled upon a post about an upcoming art exhibition in the city. She decided to take a chance and submitted some of her work for the exhibition. To her surprise, her work was accepted, and she was invited to display her art at the exhibition. The exhibition was a huge success, and Emily's work received a lot of attention. People loved her unique style and the way she portrayed emotions through her paintings. A few weeks later, a local art collector approached Emily and offered to buy one of her paintings for a significant amount of money. This was a turning point for Emily. She realized that there was a market for her art and decided to focus all her energy on her art career. She started working on new pieces and showcasing her work on social media. She even created her website to sell her artwork. Within a few months, Emily's art was in high demand, and she was receiving commissions from all over the world. She was making more money from her art than she ever thought possible, and her dreams of becoming a successful artist were finally coming true. By the end of the year, Emily had made over $200,000 from selling her art. She had quit her job at the coffee shop and was now working full-time as an artist. She felt grateful for the opportunity to pursue her passion and was determined to continue creating art that would touch people's hearts. Emily realized that with hard work and perseverance, anyone could achieve financial success. She had taken a chance and had achieved her dreams, and she was proof that anything was possible if you believe in yourself and your talents.

IV) Real estate investor

Mark had always been interested in real estate, but he had never been able to afford to buy property until he stumbled upon a unique opportunity. He had heard about a run-down apartment building in a desirable location that was up for sale at a bargain price. Mark saw the potential for the building to be renovated and turned into a luxury apartment complex. Mark knew that he didn't have enough money to buy the building himself, so he decided to partner with some friends who were also interested in real estate. They pooled their resources and bought the building. Over the next year, Mark and his friends worked tirelessly to renovate the building. They hired contractors, selected high-end finishes, and created a marketing campaign to attract tenants. It was a challenging and demanding project, but they were determined to make it a success. Their hard work paid off, and the apartment complex was a huge hit. The location, combined with the luxury finishes, made it a desirable place to live, and the apartments quickly filled up. The rental income exceeded their expectations, and they were making a significant profit each month. Mark and his partners decided to take their real estate business to the next level. They started looking for more properties to renovate and invest in. They were able to secure loans and partner with investors who were impressed with their success. Within a year, Mark and his partners had become wealthy real estate investors. They had several properties across the city, and their portfolio was growing. Mark had achieved his dream of becoming a successful real estate investor and was proud of the hard work and determination that had gotten him there. Mark realized that with the right opportunities, combined with hard work and smart investing, anyone could achieve financial success in the real estate market. He felt grateful for the opportunity to pursue his passion and was excited about what the future held for him and his partners.

V)   Fashion Business

Samantha had always been interested in fashion and had a talent for creating unique designs. However, she had never been able to turn her passion into a profitable business. One day, Samantha had an idea for a clothing line that combined her love of fashion with her desire to create sustainable and eco-friendly products. She spent months researching and designing her collection, sourcing materials that were environmentally friendly and creating a brand that reflected her values. She launched her collection online and started marketing it through social media and online advertising. To her surprise, Samantha's collection was an immediate success. People loved the unique designs and the fact that the clothing was sustainable and eco-friendly. Within a few months, Samantha had a loyal following of customers who were eagerly waiting for her next collection. Samantha worked tirelessly to grow her business, expanding her product-line and partnering with other sustainable brands. She also started offering her designs to wholesalers and boutique shops, which helped her to reach a broader audience. By the end of the year, Samantha's clothing line had become a sensation, and she had made over $1 million in sales. She had created a brand that resonated with people and was making a positive impact on the environment. Samantha realized that with hard work and dedication, anyone could achieve financial success while staying true to their values. She was proud to be making a difference in the world through her business and was determined to continue creating sustainable and eco-friendly products that people would love. Samantha's success inspired other young entrepreneurs to pursue their passions while making a positive impact on the world. She proved that it was possible to build a successful business while staying true to your values and making a difference in the world.

ABOUT THE AUTHOR

Dr. Somudeep Bhattacharjee is a distinguished author, researcher, teacher, and polymath from Tripura, India. Known for his insightful perspectives and diverse expertise, he has made significant contributions to the world of literature. Dr. Bhattacharjee writing encompasses a wide range of subjects, including finance, personal development, and success. With a focus on empowering readers, his books offer practical advice and strategies for achieving financial prosperity and personal growth. As an accomplished academic, he has published extensively in esteemed journals and academic publications. Driven by his insatiable curiosity, he explores various disciplines such as history, philosophy, and world cultures. Through his work, Dr. Bhattacharjee aims to inspire individuals to reach their full potential and attain lasting success in their lives.

THANK YOU

www.ingramcontent.com/pod-product-compliance
Lightning Source LLC
Chambersburg PA
CBHW081703220526
45466CB00009B/2862